SHAPING THE DEBATE

Defining and Discussing
HUMAN RIGHTS

DIGNITY
RESPECT
JUSTICE
FOR ALL

Christy Mihaly

Rourke
Educational Media

A Division of
Carson
Dellosa
Education

rourkeeducationalmedia.com

Before Reading: *Building Background Knowledge and Vocabulary*

Building background knowledge can help children process new information and build upon what they already know. Before reading a book, it is important to tap into what children already know about the topic. This will help them develop their vocabulary and increase their reading comprehension.

Questions and Activities to Build Background Knowledge:

1. Look at the front cover of the book and read the title. What do you think this book will be about?
2. What do you already know about this topic?
3. Take a book walk and skim the pages. Look at the table of contents, photographs, captions, and bold words. Did these text features give you any information or predictions about what you will read in this book?

Vocabulary: *Vocabulary Is Key to Reading Comprehension*

Use the following directions to prompt a conversation about each word.

- Read the vocabulary words.
- What comes to mind when you see each word?
- What do you think each word means?

> ### Vocabulary Words:
> - bipartisan
> - discrimination
> - enacted
> - entitled
> - fundamental
> - indigenous
> - inherent
> - ordinance
> - sanctions
> - scope
> - status
> - treaties

During Reading: *Reading for Meaning and Understanding*

To achieve deep comprehension of a book, children are encouraged to use close reading strategies. During reading, it is important to have children stop and make connections. These connections result in deeper analysis and understanding of a book.

 Close Reading a Text

During reading, have children stop and talk about the following:

- Any confusing parts
- Any unknown words
- Text to text, text to self, text to world connections
- The main idea in each chapter or heading

Encourage children to use context clues to determine the meaning of any unknown words. These strategies will help children learn to analyze the text more thoroughly as they read.

When you are finished reading this book, turn to page 46 for Text-Dependent Questions and an Extension Activity.

TABLE OF CONTENTS

CHAPTER ONE

WHAT ARE HUMAN RIGHTS?

Soldiers burn the homes of members of an ethnic minority and send the people fleeing from the country. Police arrest, jail, and torture participants in a peaceful protest. Factory bosses beat workers, force them to labor 16-hour shifts, and prevent them from leaving.

Torture (when pain or suffering is inflicted on a person for punishment or to get information) is a human rights abuse.

In some parts of the world, dangerous working conditions and low pay in factories violate the human rights of workers.

These actions violate people's basic human rights. In some places, local laws don't forbid such abuses. But the concept of human rights is that all people are **entitled** to fair and equal treatment, no matter what their race, gender, nationality, language, political views, sexual orientation, or religion.

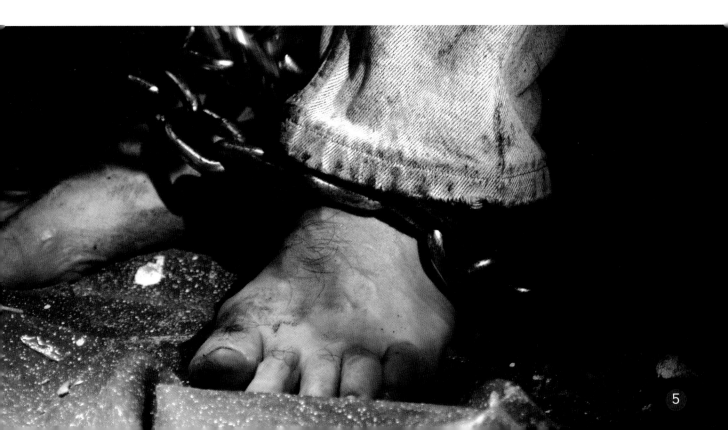

The rights not to be killed, enslaved, or tortured are human rights. The rights to self-expression and the right to clean water are often described as human rights too. But people disagree about the **scope** of these rights. For example, more than 100 nations believe killing criminals is a human rights violation and have banned executions. Other government bodies, including some states in the United States, still impose the death penalty.

This electric chair at the Florida State Prison has been used to execute condemned prisoners by electrocution.

An estimated 2.1 billion people (about 30 percent of the world's population) lack clean, safe drinking water in their homes.

Similarly, many people believe health care is a human right. Others argue that there aren't enough doctors, hospitals, and medications to treat everyone. They suggest health care should be considered a limited resource, not a right.

The United States Constitution guarantees citizens the right to vote.

Human Rights or Civil Rights?

Civil rights, such as voting rights, are rights granted by laws. The laws of different nations give different people different rights. Laws might not give non-citizens the same rights as citizens. In contrast, everyone has human rights, simply by being human. Sometimes laws and police protect human rights; sometimes they don't.

CHAPTER TWO

HUMAN RIGHTS OVER TIME

Throughout human history, people's rights depended on their **status**. Rulers had absolute power. Upper-class males had greater privileges. People could be enslaved. Yet the ancient Greeks also developed the concept of a "natural law," which applied to everyone.

This ancient Roman mosaic shows enslaved people serving others.

This stone carving depicts a slave market in ancient Egypt.

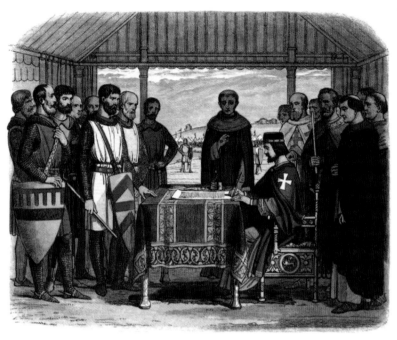

Over centuries, the notion of **fundamental** rights slowly grew. In 1215, a group of English nobles forced their king to grant them certain rights. King John signed the Magna Carta (Great Charter), limiting his own power and guaranteeing nobles the right to a fair trial and other protections.

Eight hundred years ago, the Magna Carta established that everyone, including the King, was subject to the rule of law.

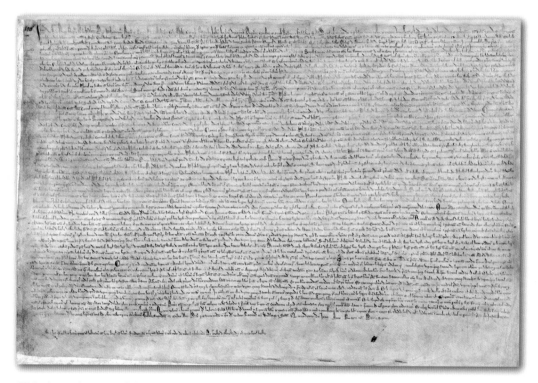

This is an image of the original 1215 Magna Carta, written in Latin.

The signers of the Declaration of Independence believed that they were entitled to the same rights guaranteed to Englishmen in the Magna Carta.

In 1776, the American colonists complained that England's King George disrespected their rights. In the Declaration of Independence, colonists explained why they rebelled against England. Their declaration stated: "All men are created equal, that they are endowed by their creator with certain unalienable rights, that among these are life, liberty and the pursuit of happiness."

Iroquois flag

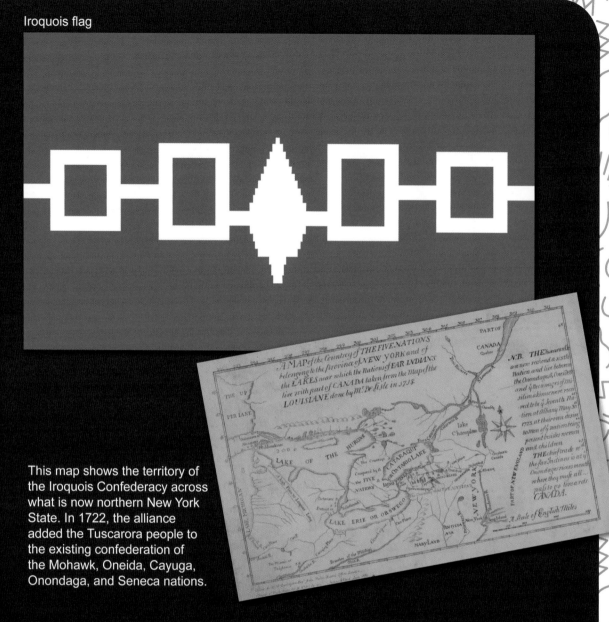

This map shows the territory of the Iroquois Confederacy across what is now northern New York State. In 1722, the alliance added the Tuscarora people to the existing confederation of the Mohawk, Oneida, Cayuga, Onondaga, and Seneca nations.

Iroquois Constitution

Before the American Revolution, the Iroquois Confederacy followed the Gayanashagowa, or Great Law of Peace. This law governed a league of five (later six) nations, specifying the leaders' duties and the rights of women and men. Benjamin Franklin and other drafters of the U.S. Constitution consulted Iroquois leaders and the Gayanashagowa.

The Nazi government under Adolf Hitler carried out a campaign of cruelty and violence and murdered millions of people in death camps.

The term *human rights* wasn't commonly used until after World War II. The brutality of that war—particularly the Nazis' mass murder of millions of Jews and "undesirables"—shocked the world. In 1945, the recovering nations joined together to form the United Nations (UN). They hoped to prevent such horrors from happening ever again. The UN aimed "to reaffirm faith in fundamental human rights, in the dignity and worth of the human person, in the equal rights of men and women…"

United Nations Member States at the End of 1945

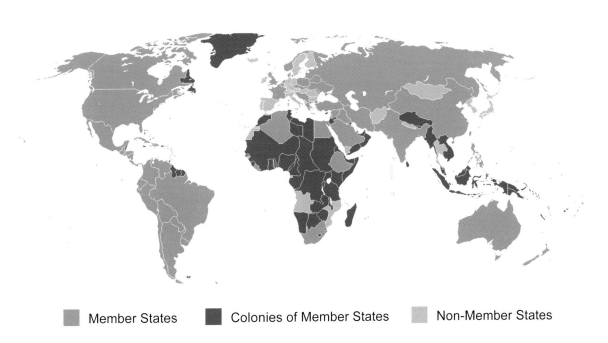

Member States   Colonies of Member States   Non-Member States

THE UNIVERSAL DECLARATION
OF Human Rights

WHEREAS recognition of the inherent dignity and of the equal and inalienable rights of all members of the human family is the foundation of freedom, justice and peace in the world,

WHEREAS disregard and contempt for human rights have resulted in barbarous acts which have outraged the conscience of mankind, and the advent of a world in which human beings shall enjoy freedom of speech and belief and freedom from fear and want has been proclaimed as the highest aspiration of the common people,

WHEREAS it is essential, if man is not to be compelled to have recourse, as a last resort, to rebellion against tyranny and oppression, that human rights should be protected by the rule of law,

WHEREAS it is essential to promote the development of friendly relations among nations,

WHEREAS the peoples of the United Nations have in the Charter reaffirmed their faith in fundamental human rights, in the dignity and worth of the human person and in the equal rights of men and women and have

determined to promote social progress and better standards of life in larger freedom,

WHEREAS Member States have pledged themselves to achieve, in co-operation with the United Nations, the promotion of universal respect for and observance of human rights and fundamental freedoms,

WHEREAS a common understanding of these rights and freedoms is of the greatest importance for the full realisation of this pledge,

NOW THEREFORE THE GENERAL ASSEMBLY

PROCLAIMS this Universal Declaration of Human Rights as a common standard of achievement for all peoples and all nations, to the end that every individual and every organ of society, keeping this Declaration constantly in mind, shall strive by teaching and education to promote respect for these rights and freedoms and by progressive measures, national and international, to secure their universal and effective recognition and observance, both among the peoples of Member States themselves and among the peoples of territories under their jurisdiction.

ARTICLE 1 —All human beings are born free and equal in dignity and rights. They are endowed with reason and conscience and should act towards one another in a spirit of brotherhood.

ARTICLE 2 —1. Everyone is entitled to all the rights and freedoms set forth in this Declaration, without distinction of any kind, such as race, colour, sex, language, religion, political or other opinion, national or social origin, property, birth or other status.

2. Furthermore, no distinction shall be made on the basis of the political, jurisdictional or international status of the country or territory to which a person belongs, whether this territory be an independent, Trust or Non-Self-Governing territory, or under any other limitation of sovereignty.

ARTICLE 3 —Everyone has the right to life, liberty and the security of person.

ARTICLE 4 —No one shall be held in slavery or servitude; slavery and the slave trade shall be prohibited in all their forms.

ARTICLE 5 —No one shall be subjected to torture or to cruel, inhuman or degrading treatment or punishment.

ARTICLE 6 —Everyone has the right to recognition everywhere as a person before the law.

ARTICLE 7 —All are equal before the law and are entitled without any discrimination to equal protection of the law. All are entitled to equal protection against any discrimination in violation of this Declaration and against any incitement to such discrimination.

ARTICLE 8 —Everyone has the right to an effective remedy by the competent national tribunals for acts violating the fundamental rights granted him by the constitution or by law.

ARTICLE 9 —No one shall be subjected to arbitrary arrest, detention or exile.

ARTICLE 10 —Everyone is entitled in full equality to a fair and public hearing by an independent and impartial tribunal, in the determination of his rights and obligations and of any criminal charge against him.

ARTICLE 11 —1. Everyone charged with a penal offence has the right to be presumed innocent until proved guilty according to law in a public trial at which he has had all the guarantees necessary for his defence.

2. No one shall be held guilty of any penal offence on account of any act or omission which did not constitute a penal offence, under national or international law, at the time when it was committed. Nor shall a heavier penalty be imposed than the one that was applicable at the time the penal offence was committed.

ARTICLE 12 —No one shall be subjected to arbitrary interference with his privacy, family, home or correspondence, nor to attacks upon his honour and reputation. Everyone has the right to the protection of the law against such interference or attacks.

ARTICLE 13 —1. Everyone has the right to freedom of movement and residence within the borders of each state.

2. Everyone has the right to leave any country, including his own, and to return to his country.

ARTICLE 14 —1. Everyone has the right to seek and to enjoy in other countries asylum from persecution.

2. This right may not be invoked in the case of prosecutions genuinely arising from non-political crimes or from acts contrary to the purposes and principles of the United Nations.

ARTICLE 15 —1. Everyone has the right to a nationality.

2. No one shall be arbitrarily deprived of his nationality nor denied the right to change his nationality.

ARTICLE 16 —1. Men and women of full age, without any limitation due to race, nationality or religion, have the right to marry and to found a family. They are entitled to equal rights as to marriage, during marriage and at its dissolution.

2. Marriage shall be entered into only with the free and full consent of the intending spouses.

3. The family is the natural and fundamental group unit of society and is entitled to protection by society and the State.

ARTICLE 17 —1. Everyone has the right to own property alone as well as in association with others.

2. No one shall be arbitrarily deprived of his property.

ARTICLE 18 —Everyone has the right to freedom of thought, conscience and religion; this right includes freedom to change his religion or belief, and freedom, either alone or in community with others and in public or private, to manifest his religion or belief in teaching, practice, worship and observance.

ARTICLE 19 —Everyone has the right to freedom of opinion and expression; this right includes freedom to hold opinions without interference and to seek, receive and impart information and ideas through any media and regardless of frontiers.

ARTICLE 20 —1. Everyone has the right to freedom of peaceful assembly and association.

2. No one may be compelled to belong to an association.

ARTICLE 21 —1. Everyone has the right to take part in the government of his country, directly or through freely chosen representatives.

2. Everyone has the right of equal access to public service in his country.

3. The will of the people shall be the basis of the authority of government; this will shall be expressed in periodic and genuine elections which shall be by universal and equal suffrage and shall be held by secret vote or by equivalent free voting procedures.

ARTICLE 22 —Everyone, as a member of society, has the right to social security and is entitled to realisation, through national effort and international co-operation and in accordance with the organisation and resources of each State, of the economic, social and cultural rights indispensable for his dignity and the free development of his personality.

ARTICLE 23 —1. Everyone has the right to work, to free choice of employment, to just and favourable conditions of work and to protection against unemployment.

2. Everyone, without any discrimination, has the right to equal pay for equal work.

3. Everyone who works has the right to just and favourable remuneration insuring for himself and his family an existence worthy of human dignity, and supplemented, if necessary, by other means of social protection.

4. Everyone has the right to form and to join trade unions for the protection of his interests.

ARTICLE 24 —Everyone has the right to rest and leisure, including reasonable limitation of working hours and periodic holidays with pay.

ARTICLE 25 —1. Everyone has the right to a standard of living adequate for the health and well-being of himself and of his family, including food, clothing, housing and medical care and necessary social services, and the right to security in the event of unemployment, sickness, disability, widowhood, old age or other lack of livelihood in circumstances beyond his control.

2. Motherhood and childhood are entitled to special care and assistance. All children, whether born in or out of wedlock, shall enjoy the same social protection.

ARTICLE 26 —1. Everyone has the right to education. Education shall be free, at least in the elementary and fundamental stages. Elementary education shall be compulsory. Technical and professional education shall be made generally available and higher education shall be equally accessible to all on the basis of merit.

2. Education shall be directed to the full development of the human personality and to the strengthening of respect for human rights and fundamental freedoms. It shall promote understanding, tolerance and friendship among all nations, racial or religious groups, and shall further the activities of the United Nations for the maintenance of peace.

3. Parents have a prior right to choose the kind of education that shall be given to their children.

ARTICLE 27 —1. Everyone has the right freely to participate in the cultural life of the community, to enjoy the arts and to share in scientific advancement and its benefits.

2. Everyone has the right to the protection of the moral and material interests resulting from any scientific, literary or artistic production of which he is the author.

ARTICLE 28 —Everyone is entitled to a social and international order in which the rights and freedoms set forth in this Declaration can be fully realized.

ARTICLE 29 —1. Everyone has duties to the community in which alone the free and full development of his personality is possible.

2. In the exercise of his rights and freedoms, everyone shall be subject only to such limitations as are determined by law solely for the purpose of securing due recognition and respect for the rights and freedoms of others and of meeting the just requirements of morality, public order and the general welfare in a democratic society.

3. These rights and freedoms may in no case be exercised contrary to the purposes and principles of the United Nations.

ARTICLE 30 —Nothing in this Declaration may be interpreted as implying for any State, group or person any right to engage in any activity or to perform any act aimed at the destruction of any of the rights and freedoms set forth herein.

UNITED NATIONS

Adopted by the United Nations General Assembly at its 183rd meeting, held in Paris on 10 December, 1948.

Issued by U.N. Department of Public Information

Article 1 of the UDHR states: "All human beings are born free and equal in dignity and rights."

In 1948, the UN adopted the Universal Declaration of Human Rights (UDHR), recognizing all people's **inherent** rights. The UDHR lists numerous rights, including the rights to life, liberty, safety, education, work, and fair pay. It proclaims there should be no slavery, torture, or arrest without cause. It declares everyone should have freedom of thought, freedom of movement, and freedom to assemble peacefully. It has been translated into 500 languages.

Drafting the UDHR

The committee of the UN Commission on Human Rights that drafted the UDHR included members from various political, cultural, and religious traditions. The committee chair, former U.S. first lady Eleanor Roosevelt, pushed to find common ground that all could endorse. The group came together to support universal freedom from oppression.

CHAPTER THREE

EXPANDING RIGHTS IN THE UNITED STATES

The U.S. Constitution as originally **enacted** focused on the structure of the government. In 1791, the Bill of Rights—the first ten amendments to the Constitution—was added to specify the rights of individuals. These amendments guarantee freedom of speech, freedom from cruel and unusual punishment, and other important rights. Yet not all Americans enjoyed these rights equally.

In 1789, Congress forwarded to the state legislatures twelve proposed constitutional amendments that would expressly protect Americans' individual rights. Ten of these amendments were approved by the states and added to the Constitution in 1791.

In 1863, Congressman James Mitchell Ashley introduced the legislation that eventually became the 13th Amendment, abolishing slavery.

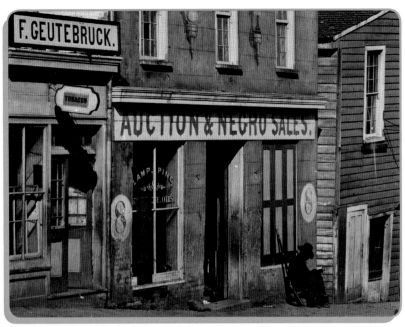

A man with a rifle sits outside an Atlanta slave market in this 1864 photograph.

In the 1780s, more than 15 percent of Americans were enslaved. Slavery continued until the Civil War ended in 1865. After the war, three amendments were added to the Constitution. The 13th Amendment outlawed slavery.

This photograph is attributed to Timothy H. O'Sullivan and dated 1862. It is said to portray a group of more than 100 people liberated by the Union Army during the Civil War, standing by their former slave quarters on a South Carolina cotton plantation.

The 14th Amendment promised everyone equal protection of the laws. The 15th guaranteed voting rights to male citizens regardless of race.

On March 31, 1870, Thomas Mundy Peterson became the first African American to vote after the passage of the 15th Amendment. He cast his ballot in a local election in Perth Amboy, New Jersey.

This print from 1870 celebrates African Americans' post-Civil War achievements and the passage of the 15th Amendment.

Kanye West and the 13th Amendment

The 13th Amendment prohibits slavery or involuntary servitude "except as a punishment for crime." Rapper Kanye West argued in 2018 that this language allows convicted prisoners to be forced to work—essentially treated as slaves. He called for revising the amendment to prohibit forced prison labor.

Kanye West is a hip-hop artist and songwriter known for speaking his mind.

Many Americans continued to face **discrimination** and unequal treatment. For example, the government didn't grant women the right to vote until 1920. Lesbian, gay, bisexual, and transgender (LGBT) people could be sent to psychiatric hospitals based on their sexual orientation or gender identity. Others, including African Americans, immigrants, American Indians, and people with disabilities also were deprived of equal rights.

The campaign for women's suffrage, or the right to vote, took many years of effort.

Sculptor George Segal created "Gay Liberation" in Greenwich Village, New York City, to honor the fight for LGBT equality. The sculpture, bronze with white lacquer, was dedicated in 1992.

Jim Crow laws meant separate water for white people and black people.

Segregated waiting areas were a feature of the Durham, North Carolina, bus station, shown in this photo from 1940.

Jim Crow Laws

After the Civil War, "Jim Crow" laws in southern states enforced racial segregation. Until the 1950s and 1960s, African Americans attended separate, inferior schools and were forbidden from using "whites-only" restrooms, libraries, restaurants, pools, drinking fountains, parks, and other public facilities. They were often prevented from owning property or voting.

Americans organized and pushed for equality. They challenged segregated schools. In 1954, the Supreme Court struck down public school segregation in *Brown v. Board of Education*. In the civil rights movement of the 1960s, African Americans demanded equal treatment. Congress responded with new laws. The Civil Rights Act of 1964 outlawed discrimination based on race, religion, sex, or national origin.

In March 1964, Martin Luther King, Jr. and Malcolm X both went to the U.S. Capitol to hear the Senate debate on the bill that would become the Civil Rights Act of 1964.

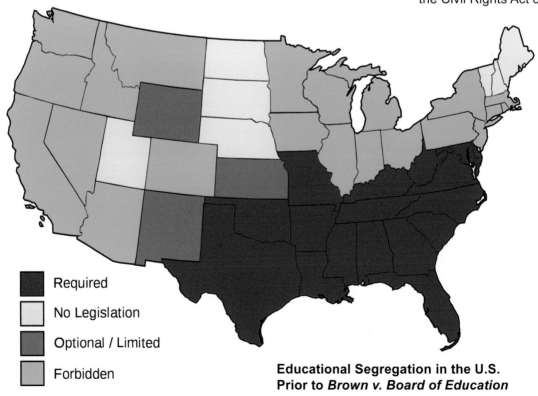

Required

No Legislation

Optional / Limited

Forbidden

Educational Segregation in the U.S. Prior to *Brown v. Board of Education*

U.S. President Lyndon B. Johnson signed the Civil Rights Act of 1964 in a ceremony attended by Martin Luther King, Jr. and many others.

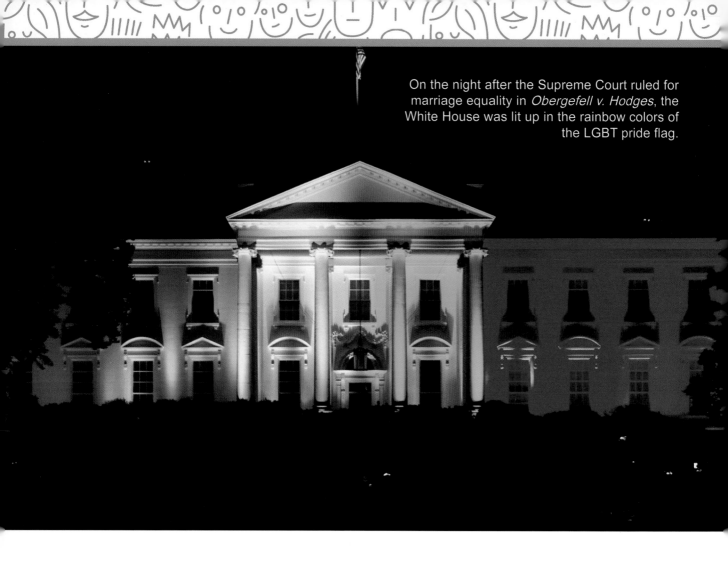

On the night after the Supreme Court ruled for marriage equality in *Obergefell v. Hodges*, the White House was lit up in the rainbow colors of the LGBT pride flag.

The 1968 Indian Civil Rights Act protected the rights of American Indians. In 1990, the Americans with Disabilities Act prohibited discrimination against people with disabilities.

People also went to court to defend their rights. In the 1967 case *Loving v. Virginia*, Richard and Mildred Loving challenged a Virginia law that said a person could not marry someone of another race. The Supreme Court overturned the law, declaring Americans have the freedom to marry. Almost 50 years later, in the 2015 *Obergefell v. Hodges* ruling, the Supreme Court established that the right to marry extends to same-sex couples.

CHAPTER FOUR

INTERNATIONAL HUMAN RIGHTS

Some governments severely limit their people's rights. Oppressive governments shut down hospitals, schools, and news organizations, and allow rulers to get richer while the people live in poverty. People are arrested for their sexual orientation or membership in political organizations. Critics of government policies are exiled or killed.

In reaction to such human rights violations, other nations may punish the offending government. They may withdraw aid or refuse to do business with a country that abuses its people. Sometimes this pressure persuades government leaders to respect human rights. Often, however, one country's leaders won't interfere in another country's affairs. Some argue that different cultures have different notions of rights, and that these differences should be respected.

Fighting for Her Rights

In 2012, Samar Badawi received an International Women of Courage Award from the U.S. State Department.

In Saudi Arabia, women need a male guardian's permission to marry. In 2010, Samar Badawi sued her father for withholding his permission. She won the right to marry, and later fought for women's rights to vote and to drive cars. In July 2018, she was arrested, apparently for her activism.

President Bashar al-Assad blamed rebel forces for chemical weapons attacks during the Syrian Civil War.

To protect human rights cooperatively, countries enter into **treaties**. For example, treaties banning chemical weapons have resulted in the destruction of most of the world's chemical weapons. However, agreements cannot always prevent problems. Poison gas was used in Syria's civil war, and UN investigators concluded the government of Syrian President Bashar al-Assad was responsible. Some nations imposed financial **sanctions** against Syria, but Russia defended Syria and blocked a coordinated international response.

The UN Human Rights Committee has urged an end to the use of weapons of mass destruction (nuclear and chemical weapons).

Human rights advocates pay special attention to refugees—those who have left their home countries fleeing dangers or persecution. The UN works with governments and aid organizations to assist the world's 25 million refugees, along with another 40 million people who are displaced within their own countries. These people are homeless and often in dire need.

During the Syrian Civil War, which started in 2011, millions of people fled to seek refuge in other countries.

Many Syrians who sought safety in Turkey ended up confined to refugee camps.

For instance, more than 700,000 Rohingya people have fled from Myanmar and are living in refugee camps. The Rohingya, a Muslim minority in predominately Buddhist Myanmar, had long been mistreated. In 2017, thousands began fleeing Myanmar after the army killed Rohingya people and burned their villages. A UN investigation was launched to consider criminal charges against those responsible. Meanwhile, aid groups provided food and medical help to the Rohingya, as their future remained uncertain.

Many thousands of Rohingya people were pushed into refugee camps in Bangladesh.

Laws about human rights respond to changing situations. For example, because air and water pollution make people ill, courts have recognized a human right to environmental protection. In 2018, the Inter-American Court of Human Rights declared, "A clean environment is a fundamental right for the existence of humanity."

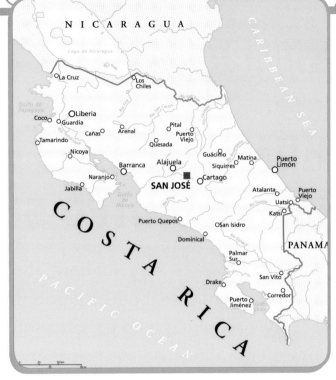

The Inter-American Court of Human Rights is based in San José, Costa Rica. It hears cases regarding accusations of human rights violations by members of the Organization of American States (OAS), which is made up of the nations of North, Central, and South America.

Around the globe, laws about air pollution vary between countries. An estimated 90 percent of people on Earth breathe air that is polluted and unhealthy.

CHAPTER FIVE

HUMAN RIGHTS CHALLENGES IN THE UNITED STATES

President Donald Trump said the First Step Act would "provide hope and a second chance, to those who earn it."

Although some may not care about criminals' rights, advocates argue that harsh U.S. laws requiring long prison sentences for nonviolent crimes violate prisoners' human rights. These laws also result in racial injustice because people of color are arrested and incarcerated at higher rates than whites, especially for drug offenses. Republicans and Democrats came together in December 2018 to enact **bipartisan** reforms. Congress passed, and President Trump signed, the First Step Act, which shortened sentences and expanded job training and other measures to reduce jail time and improve people's lives after prison.

Indigenous communities from throughout North America protested the Dakota Access Pipeline, rallying around the slogan, "Water Is Life!"

Dakota Access Pipeline: Human Rights Versus Corporate Rights

In 2016, Sioux tribal members and supporters opposed an oil pipeline that they said threatened to contaminate their water. Thousands demonstrated at Standing Rock Reservation, North Dakota. They failed to stop the pipeline. But they brought worldwide attention to environmental and human rights—especially of **indigenous** peoples—threatened by construction projects.

The Dakota Access Pipeline runs southeast from North Dakota's Bakken oil fields, along the edge of the Standing Rock Reservation (shown in orange), across South Dakota and Iowa, to an oil facility in Illinois.

To protect LGBT rights, laws prohibit discrimination based on sexual orientation or gender identity. Some interest groups argue that this infringes on their religious freedoms. For example, if a florist says her religion opposes same-sex marriage, must she nonetheless sell wedding flowers to same-sex couples? It's an area of ongoing debate.

Transgender people, who identify as a gender other than that assigned at birth, also seek equal rights—and face opposition. In 2016, the city of Charlotte, North Carolina, passed an **ordinance** allowing people to use public restrooms of the gender with which they identify. City leaders sought to assure equal access and safety for transgender people.

New signs mark bathrooms for transgender people and people with disabilities.

The North Carolina state legislature opposed Charlotte's ordinance and enacted a state law, House Bill 2 (HB2), in response. HB2 required people to use only restrooms matching the sex on their birth certificate. Its supporters argued that women and girls might feel threatened if a transgender woman (identified as male at birth) entered their restroom. They worried about sexual assault. Researchers have concluded, however, that there is no evidence that transgender access increases crimes in bathrooms.

LGBT activists challenged HB2. Companies and athletic organizations also canceled events in North Carolina and refused to do business there. This boycott cost the state and its businesses hundreds of thousands of dollars. North Carolina repealed HB2 in 2017, but the legislature said the discussion would continue.

Protesters rallied against North Carolina's HB2 as a violation of the rights of transgender people.

Poverty and Homelessness in the U.S.

The Universal Declaration of Human Rights (UDHR) lists food, housing, and basic support as human rights. The U.S. homeless population was more than 550,000 in 2018. Recent UN reports condemn U.S. failure to provide housing and food to needy Americans. "The situation is unacceptable in light of the wealth of the country," said one UN investigator.

CHAPTER SIX

AMERICA'S ROLE IN THE WORLD

The United States has often promoted international human rights. It has demanded that other nations protect their citizens' human rights before doing business with the U.S. For instance, for many years, the U.S. protested Cuba's human rights violations by restricting trade with Cuba.

Examples of United States Sanctions

Country		Reasons for Sanctions Include
Iran		Iran's record of serious human rights violations, and a nuclear program that could lead to development of nuclear weapons
North Korea		North Korea's extreme human rights abuses, cyber attacks on United States computer systems, and an aggressive nuclear weapons program
Syria		Syria's record of serious human rights violations, and additional abuses by the government in the Syrian Civil War
Cuba		Cuba's record of human rights violations, and United States financial claims against the Cuban government
Venezuela		Venezuela's poor human rights record and public corruption

In other cases, U.S. leaders have reacted differently. One example was the 2018 murder of Jamal Khashoggi, a journalist critical of Saudi Arabia's Crown Prince Mohammed bin Salman. A U.S. investigation concluded the crown prince had likely ordered the murder. President Donald Trump did not impose sanctions on Saudi Arabia, saying it would be foolish to cancel billions of dollars worth of contracts with that country. In response, the Senate voted unanimously to oppose Trump's position and to hold Mohammed bin Salman responsible for the murder.

Mohammed bin Salman, widely known as "MBS," is the heir to the throne of Saudi Arabia and has been criticized for human rights abuses.

Jamal Khashoggi was a well-known Saudi journalist and advocate of a free press who left Saudi Arabia because he feared being arrested.

Do Consumer Boycotts Improve Working Conditions?

Some U.S. consumers won't buy goods made in sweatshops—factories in developing countries where workers receive low pay in dangerous conditions. Economists say if sweatshops close, workers will have worse jobs, or none. They suggest a campaign to pressure companies to improve working conditions would be better than a boycott.

President Barack Obama signed an executive order calling on the military to close Guantanamo Bay prison camp, but President Trump later ordered the camp to remain open.

The United States itself stands accused of violating international human rights. The U.S. imprisoned hundreds of suspected terrorists at Guantanamo Bay prison camp in Cuba after the September 11, 2001 attacks on the United States. Prisoners were held without trial; some were tortured. In 2018, American actions at the Mexico-U.S. border, separating children from parents, were widely condemned. And many people criticize the United States's death penalty, police shootings of unarmed people, and harsh treatment of needy and homeless people.

Law enforcement officers monitor the U.S.-Mexico international border. Parts of the border are marked by barriers such as this section between San Diego, California, and Tijuana, Mexico.

In 2017 and 2018, large migrant caravans, mostly women and children from Central America, banded together for safety on their trip to the United States. They were fleeing gang violence and seeking U.S. asylum.

The Right to Seek Asylum

Immigrants have the right to seek asylum—safety—when fleeing persecution in their home countries. In 2018, President Trump declared that people crossing the border illegally were ineligible for asylum. Human rights lawyers said this policy violated U.S. law. Calling asylum-seekers "criminals," Trump continued efforts to restrict asylum rights.

In 2018, U.S. Ambassador to the UN Nikki Haley announced the U.S. was quitting the UN Human Rights Council. She said the council was biased in criticizing some countries (such as Israel) but not others (such as China). Haley added that the United States remains committed to defending human rights around the world.

Before serving as the Trump administration's representative to the UN, Nikki Haley was governor of South Carolina from 2011 to 2017.

Nikki Haley (left) and U.S. Secretary of State Mike Pompeo discussed the 2018 decision of the United States to leave the Human Rights Council.

The United States and Human Rights

As President John F. Kennedy reminded the nation in a famous 1963 speech about civil rights, the United States was "founded on the principle that all men are created equal, and that the rights of every man are diminished when the rights of one man are threatened."

In his televised June 1963 address to the nation, President Kennedy called on Congress to enact laws "giving all Americans the right to be served in facilities which are open to the public," and to end the rule of Jim Crow.

PRACTICE PREPARING FOR A DEBATE

People explain issues and solve problems through discussion. Debates are formal discussions about an issue. Debate participants present facts they have gathered from reliable sources. They present this information as they try to convince listeners that their opinions about an issue are correct.

Supplies

- paper
- pencil
- books on your topic and/or internet access

Directions:

1. Decide the topic you will research.

2. Write a question that will shape your debate. Example: Should religion be taught in public schools?

3. Write your proposition or opposition statement. Proposition example: Religion should be taught in public schools. Opposition example: Religion should not be taught in public schools.

4. Research your topic using a variety of sources. Make a list of the facts you find and note the source of each fact next to it.

5. Practice presenting your argument.

6. Flip the script! Follow steps 1–5 again, this time preparing with facts that support the other side.

Bonus: Form a debate club with your friends. Assign a new topic regularly. Give each person equal time to present their arguments.

Glossary

bipartisan (bye-PAR-tuh-suhn): involving the agreement of two political parties that usually oppose one another

discrimination (dis-krim-i-NAY-shuhn): unfair conduct toward others based on differences in race, gender, religion, age, and the like

enacted (en-AC-tid): made something a law

entitled (en-TYE-tuhld): having a right to something

fundamental (fuhn-duh-MEN-tuhl): basic or important

indigenous (in-DIJ-uh-nuhs): native to or originating in a particular place

inherent (in-HAIR-uhnt): a natural, characteristic part of something

ordinance (OR-duh-nuhns): a law or regulation of a town or city

sanctions (SANGK-shuhnz): punishments, especially of one nation against another

scope (skohp): area or range of operation

status (STA-tuhs): rank or position in a group or society

treaties (TREE-teez): formal written agreements between countries

Index

Text-Dependent Questions

1. What are some laws and court cases that protect human rights in the United States?

2. How did World War II affect the modern concept of human rights?

3. What are some ways in which the U.S. government may have violated human rights?

4. How does the United Nations defend human rights?

5. Name an example of a current human rights conflict in the United States.

Extension Activity

Imagine you work for the mayor of a city with a growing homeless population. People are living in tents, using hoses for water, and cooking over fires in a public park. The park's bathroom is out of order. Nearby residents complain about the tents, fires, noise, and waste in the park, and their fear of crime. The mayor asks you for recommendations. Write a report considering the complaints and the rights of the homeless people and advising the mayor on what the city should do.

Bibliography

Alston, Philip, "Statement on Visit to the USA." United Nations, Human Rights, Office of the High Commissioner, Dec. 15, 2017. https://www.ohchr.org/EN/NewsEvents/Pages/DisplayNews.aspx?NewsID=22533.

Bendix, Aria, "UN Expert: San Francisco's Homelessness Crisis Is a Human Rights Violation and Suggests 'A Cruelty That Is Unsurpassed.'" *Business Insider*, Nov. 12, 2018. https://www.businessinsider.com/un-expert-san-francisco-homeless-cruelty-2018-11.

Fandos, Nicholas, "Senate Passes Bipartisan Criminal Justice Bill." *The New York Times*, Dec. 18, 2018. https://www.nytimes.com/2018/12/18/us/politics/senate-criminal-justice-bill.html.

France, Lisa Respers, "Kanye West Explains His 13th Amendment Comments." CNN Entertainment, Oct. 2, 2018. https://www.cnn.com/2018/10/02/entertainment/kanye-west-13th-amendment-clarification/index.html.

Hughes, Rebecca, "8 Women Who Used Activism to Fight for Human Rights in 2018." *The Lily*, Nov. 30, 2018. https://www.thelily.com/8-women-who-used-activism-to-fight-for-human-rights-in-2018/.

Human Rights Watch, World Report 2018: Our annual review of human rights around the globe. https://www.hrw.org/world-report/2018. Accessed December 29, 2018.

Musalo, Karen, "When Rights and Cultures Collide." Markkula Center for Applied Ethics at Santa Clara University. https://www.scu.edu/ethics/ethics-resources/ethical-decision-making/when-rights-and-cultures-collide/. Last updated Nov. 12, 2015.

National Park Service, "Telling All Americans' Stories." https://www.nps.gov/subjects/tellingallamericansstories/index.htm. Accessed Dec. 29, 2018.

Orellana, Marcos, "Court Embraces Right to a Healthy Environment in the Americas." Human Rights Watch, Feb. 14, 2018. https://www.hrw.org/news/2018/02/14/court-embraces-right-healthy-environment-americas.

United Nations, "Human Rights." http://www.un.org/en/sections/issues-depth/human-rights/. Accessed December 29, 2018.

United Nations, "Universal Declaration of Human Rights." http://www.un.org/en/universal-declaration-human-rights/index.html. (accessed Dec. 29, 2018).

United States State Department, "Bureau of Democracy, Human Rights, and Labor." https://www.state.gov/j/drl/. Accessed December 29, 2018.

About the Author

Christy Mihaly writes books, articles, poetry, and stories. She earned degrees in policy studies and law, and worked as an attorney for two decades before becoming an author. She has lived in Spain, and spent time in a variety of places including Brazil, China, Honduras, India, Mexico, Morocco, New Zealand, and the Philippines. Visit her at www.christymihaly.com.

www.rourkeeducationalmedia.com

PHOTO CREDITS: Cover © Editorial Credit Ken Wolter / Shutterstock.com, drawings of faces © topform; pages 4-5 interrogation © Sergey Petrov, chained feet © Luisa Leal Photography, factory workers © xiao yu; pages 6-7 drinking water © Riccardo Mayer, baby © Oksana Kuzmina, hospital © Chaikom, pages 8-9 voters © Burlingham; page 19 © Editorial Credit: Featureflash Photo Agency; page 20 sculptures in Christopher Par, NYC © Editorial Credit: poludziber; page 27 refugee camp © Editorial Credit: thomas koch, Syrian refugees arriving in Greece by dinghy © Editorial credit: Anjo Kan; page 29 map © Peter Hermes Furian, photo © Tatiana Grozetskaya; page 30 © Editorial credit: Joseph Sohm, page 31 protesters © Editorial credit: arindambanerjee; page 32 flag © Africa Studio, brides © cunaplus; pages 34-35 © Editorial credit: protesters © J. Bicking; page 36 homeless man © Editorial credit: Joseph Sohm, page 37 flags: Iran © dovla982; North Korea © G7 Stock; Cuba © N.Vector Design; Syria © Peter Probst, Sudan © Rvector, Venezuela © Gil C; page 38 image of Prince Mohammed bin Salman © Editorial credit: Friemann, page 39 factory workers © Editorial credit: catastrophe_OL; Page 40-41 border patrol © Sherry V Smith, child with water bottle © Editorial credit: Vic Hinterlang, protesters © Editorial credit: Karl_Sonnenberg, page 41 Honduran women and children in truck © Editorial credit: Vic Hinterlang All images from Shutterstock.com except pages 6-7 electric chair courtesy of Florida Department of Corrections/Doug Smith. page 9 Roman mosaic © Pascal Radigue https://creativecommons.org/licenses/by/3.0/deed.en ; Egyptian carving © Mike Knell https://creativecommons.org/licenses/by-sa/2.0/ page 10 King John signing Magna Carta Public Domain image 1864; page 12 Iroquois flag Public Domain image, author: Zscout370; page 13 map Public Domain image, author: Clam15; page 14 courtesy of United Nations Department of Public Information; page 16 Bill of Rights courtesy of National Archives and Records Administration, page 17 Slave Market courtesy of Library of Congress, group of freed slaves public domain image, Wikimedia, Representative James Mitchell Ashley courtesy of Library of Congress; page 18 "Celebrating the Fifteenth Amendment" and page 20 Woman Suffrage Headquarters, page 21 colored waiting room and drinking fountain photos, pages 22-23 Martin Luther King and Malcolm X courtesy of The Library of Congress, page 22 map by King of Hearts https://creativecommons.org/licenses/by-sa/3.0/deed.en , signing of the 1964 Civil Rights Act courtesy of U.S. federal government, Page 24 Whitehouse © Ted Eytan https://creativecommons.org/licenses/by-sa/2.0/ ; page 26 President Bashar al-Assad © Kremlin.ru https://creativecommons.org/licenses/by/4.0/deed.en Weapons of Mass Destruction art © Fastfission https://creativecommons.org/licenses/by-sa/3.0/deed.en; page 28 © DFID - UK Department for International Development https://creativecommons.org/licenses/by-sa/2.0/deed.en, Page 30 President Trump courtesy of U.S. federal government; page 31 © NittyG https://creativecommons.org/licenses/by-sa/4.0/deed.en; page 33 public restroom sign © Kaldari Page 38 Jamal Khashoggi © April Brady / POMED https://creativecommons.org/licenses/by/2.0/deed.en, Page 40 Camp Delta Photo by Kathleen T. Rhem/U.S. Military; Page 42 and 43 photos courtesy of the U.S. Federal Government

Edited by: Kim Thompson
Produced by Blue Door Education for Rourke Educational Media. Cover and interior design by: Jennifer Dydyk

Library of Congress PCN Data

Defining and Discussing Human Rights / Christy Mihaly
(Shaping the Debate)
ISBN 978-1-73161-472-8 (hard cover)
ISBN 978-1-73161-279-3 (soft cover)
ISBN 978-1-73161-577-0 (e-Book)
ISBN 978-1-73161-682-1 (e-Pub)
Library of Congress Control Number: 2019932390

Rourke Educational Media
Printed in the United States of America,
North Mankato, Minnesota